METANOIA

[meh-ta-noy-ah] • Greek

(n.) the journey of changing one's mind, heart, self, or way of life; spiritual conversion.

By: Lani Gonzales

Copyright © 2024 by Lani Gonzales.

All rights reserved. Printed in the United States of America. No part of this book may be used or reproduced in any manner whatsoever without written permission except in the case of brief quotations embodied in critical articles or reviews.

www.AdAstraAwakening.com

First Edition: August 15, 2024

Author's Biography

Lani Gonzales is a powerhouse of inspiration, using her light as a beacon to guide others towards theirs. After immigrating to the United States with her family when she was only two years old, Lani adopted her parents' discipline and ambition, working through college and law school to become a partner at a successful law firm in Tampa, Florida. Realizing that her heart was called to serve, Lani took a leap of faith and started her wellness practice, Ad Astra Awakening. Now a clinical hypnotherapist, Lani has blazed a trail of holistic self-discovery and is committed to helping others live passionate, purposeful, soul-driven lives.

Dedication

To all the places and people around the world
that healed my heart as I journeyed *home*.

To the family and friends who stand with me in this lifetime,
not allowing me to stay small.

To those who feel lost in the dark.
You are the light.

Introduction

I grew up on fairytales and stories of happily ever after, and I dreamed of one day having my own love story. After decades of broken hearts and broken dreams, after countless cycles of remembering, forgetting, and remembering again the truth of who I am, I found myself in the center of the greatest love story.

It's the kind of love story not often told and too easily overlooked. There is no princess. No meet cute. No knight in shining armor. It is nonetheless a tale of fervent love.

Love of seemingly ordinary people who shared their wisdom, teaching me what it truly meant to live. Love of sights, smells, and sounds that awakened my senses to the beauty found in every facet of existence. Love of every step of the journey, the constant unearthing of who we truly are.

This story is my rebellion against happily ever after—the picture-perfect life sold in fairytales, movies, and social media. At the end of this book, there is no happily ever after. Instead, I leave you with something greater: passion, purpose, and truth ever after.

Table of Contents

Chapter 1: The End	1
Chapter 2: Broken	3
Chapter 3: Recalculating	4
Chapter 4: The Suitcase	7
Chapter 5: Monks, Elephants, and Ping Pong Balls	11
Chapter 6: Dolphins and Drug Dealers	16
Chapter 7: Sensations	22
Chapter 8: Flamenco and Fire	27
Chapter 9: The Shit and the Shaman	30
Chapter 10: The Place Where Things Are Made	39
Chapter 11: The Remembering	49
Chapter 12: Breath	54
Chapter 13: God	58
Chapter 14: The Calling	63
Chapter 15: The Beginning	68
Epilogue	76

Chapter 1
The End

It was the end of the world. At least, the end of the world as I knew it.

I had my life perfectly planned. Shaped by the uncertainty and struggles of immigrating to America with my family at two years old, I decided early on that the only way to avoid drowning in the chaos of life was to have a plan. College. Law school. Partner at a law firm. Married by the age of thirty. Two children by the age of thirty-five. I knew the exact trajectory and timeline of my life.

But at the age of twenty-seven, my world crumbled. I pursued my career relentlessly, determined to be a successful, self-made woman in the male-dominated arena of law. But as I worked in my office in Tampa, Florida, minutes passed, at seven p.m., a voice within me screamed, *What am I doing?*

I tried to continue working, but the question haunted me. "What am I doing?"

Friends, family, and peers admired my hustle, my drive to succeed. But as I sat in my office that evening, I realized that I had driven too quickly through life, blindly going through the motions and milestones just to check a box off my *perfect* life plan. That evening in my office, I finally found a moment of stillness. I sat in silence, trying to dissect the life choices that brought me to that chair and that office past seven p.m. I tried to determine whether I was happy, whether I even knew what happiness truly was.

For hours, I sat in silence, surrounded by volumes of my law school textbooks. I had graduated from law school five years before, the information in the textbooks no longer useful, but I was still bound to them by thirty years of student loan payments. I couldn't bear the thought of discarding something that I had invested in so greatly.

I had dumped thousands of dollars into the textbooks that surrounded me, hundreds of hours to create my career, and decades of hard work to bring my *perfect* life plan to fruition. But they no longer served me. My bank account was full, but my life felt empty.

I began to explore the recesses of my emptiness and the parts of my life built by blindly going through the motions. The same voice inside me that interrupted my work whispered, *Mick.* After dating Mick for seven years, the milestones of my *perfect* life plan included marrying him, buying a house, and starting a family. But as the illusions of my life shattered, so did my dream of marrying Mick. We didn't share the same values or goals. All we shared was fond memories and the unwillingness to let seven years of love go to waste.

Still sitting in the stillness, I realized that I was clinging to more than just the armrest of my office chair. I clung to a job, a relationship, and an empty life simply for the sake of safety and security. I had latched onto a life that lacked passion for the comfort of predictability and certainty.

I stood from my chair, finally breaking the stillness, and as I walked out of my office with my ideal list torn to pieces, only one thing was certain: happiness did not exist within the confines of my *perfect* life plan.

Chapter 2
Broken

Despite following my life plan with precision, I was now single, heartbroken, and unfulfilled. Without the guideposts and milestones of my former design, I drowned in the darkness of depression. My perfect life plan failed to account for the detours of shattered dreams and a broken heart.

Some days, I sobbed. Escaping the world from the fortress of my bed, I hid beneath blankets and pillows, accompanied only by the tear-soaked tissues littered around me and empty ice cream pints. I ached for a new and better day to come, only to be disappointed when each day started with unrelenting pain in my heart and a knot in the pit of my stomach.

Some days, I strived. I poured what was left of me into marathons, triathlons, and competitive martial arts. I hoped that with each achievement, award, or trophy, I could fill the hollowness within me. But as I stood on podiums and crossed finish lines, the satisfaction I found quickly fled. I couldn't escape. The emptiness inside me lingered.

Some days, I gave way to my grief. Some days, I hid behind my armor and a smile that seemed to convince the people around me that all was well. But every day, every single day, I felt broken.

Chapter 3
Recalculating

It was one of those rainy Mondays, the kind where the sky can't decide whether to cry or just grumble. Same route, same job, same rinse-and-repeat routine that left my soul feeling like an empty shell. But that day, as my car drove along to the office, my mind took a detour down the path of "what if." What if life could be different? What if there was more? What if I was more?

Lost in thought, I missed my highway exit to downtown Tampa. The GPS chimed in with a robotic "recalculating." I kept driving, winding through streets and avenues, each recalculated turn sparking another thought of "what if." The GPS never said I was lost, just rerouting. It made me think—what if life is like that too? What if our paths can always be recalculated?

"What if" transformed from a question into a declaration of intent.

…

The next Monday, I set my GPS for Miami, Florida, back to where my journey into the "real world" began, hoping to understand why my perfectly planned life felt like a failure. Memories flooded back during the four-hour drive of me at eighteen, my car packed with clothes and dreams, moving from a quiet Virginia suburb to the vibrant chaos of college life in Miami. I was terrified but determined to "be somebody."

In Miami, I had declared not just my college major but also my disbelief in God. God never saved me from rape or abuse. It felt impossible to believe in a God who refused to answer my only childhood prayer: to make the pain go away. I spent my childhood singing in the church choir, hiding my disdain for God and religion behind hymns and rote prayers. At eighteen, I finally cast off that mask, a liberation that felt like betrayal to my devout Christian parents.

During college, I rented a room from Sheila, a woman who, at first glance, seemed ordinary, with her dirty blonde hair and Midwestern warmth. But Sheila was anything but ordinary. She was freshly divorced, and I was fresh into college. Despite the age gap, we bonded over triathlons and our shared status as black sheep of our families. She became more than a landlord—she became my family.

There were times when I borrowed Sheila's hope and times when she borrowed mine. She assured me that all parents love their children, even when I felt unloved. She promised that hard work would pay off, and she was right. Although I had checked off "successful lawyer" from my perfect life plan, somehow, I felt hollow. With my life in shambles and a heart echoing with emptiness, I visited Sheila, hoping she could help me piece it all back together.

We sat at her kitchen table, the same one where I once pored over textbooks and dreams. I sobbed about my failures, and Sheila's eyes, filled with unwavering affection, were a sanctuary amid the chaos. My silent questions hung in the air: Was it all a waste? Am I irretrievably lost? Am I irreparably broken?

Too afraid to voice them, I simply asked, "What do I do now?"

Sheila's eyes sparkled with a secret she seemed eager to share. "Travel. You should travel," she said.

"What?" I stammered. "My career is crumbling. My love life is a mess. Everything is falling apart, and you think I should leave?"

Sheila nodded, offering no further explanation. The "why" was mine to discover.

"How about Guatemala?" she suggested. "It's my happy place. Maybe it'll help you find yours. Maybe even God."

I scoffed. Finding myself was challenging enough without seeking some guy in the sky. While I didn't believe in God, I did believe in Sheila. Despite her own struggles, something within her remained unscathed—a fire that burned with resilience and strength.

Open to finding that fire within myself, I considered her advice. "I speak Spanish like a toddler. How could I possibly travel to Guatemala?"

Sheila smiled. "You can go anywhere in the world as long as you have two things: patience and a sense of humor."

With what patience and humor I could muster, I purchased a plane ticket to Guatemala.

Chapter 4
The Suitcase

In my characteristic "stay in control" fashion, I devoured travel books, marked them up, and plotted out every inch of my trip to Guatemala. I was a woman on a mission, yet fear and uncertainty hung around like unwanted guests. My overstuffed suitcase was a perfect metaphor for my apprehensions. Packed tight with clothes for any conceivable situation, it was my attempt to outsmart fate by preparing for the unpredictable.

The plan was perfect until I met my first challenge: dragging a fifty-pound suitcase through a dirt trail up a dormant volcano. I wrestled with my luggage along a steep, winding path as the stunning view of Lake Atitlán unfolded before me, a shimmering mirror framed by rugged terrain and majestic volcanoes. Volcán Atitlán stood tall, whispering ancient secrets. Volcán Tolimán radiated quiet strength, while Volcán San Pedro, with its lush green slopes, beckoned hikers to its summit, mirroring my own uphill battle. As I trudged along, the landscape unfurled like a living painting.

Just when I thought my strength might give out, a friendly face emerged from the foliage—a young man from the Isla Verde Ecological Retreat. He offered to carry my suitcase the rest of the way. I accepted with heaving gratitude.

"Your suitcase has more clothes than a Guatemalan family," he joked. We both laughed, sharing the weight and the journey. His kindness and the awe-inspiring surroundings turned the last leg of the climb into a shared adventure. Even in unfamiliar territory, a stranger's kindness can lighten the world's weight.

In my cabin, cooled by the crisp air scented with pine and earth, I watched the sunset paint the sky in shades of orange and pink. As night fell, the peak of a volcano glowed faintly, dancing with the twinkling stars. I drifted off to sleep, unsure of the future but hopeful this journey might help me find my way—or better yet, myself.

Morning broke over the Guatemalan highlands, casting a golden glow upon Lake Atitlán. Each day, I explored the towns around the lake. In San Pedro La Laguna, I walked cobbled streets, admiring vibrant murals that told stories of Mayan culture. Locals bustled about with smiles that radiated the joy of living amidst such natural splendor. Hiking through lush coffee plantations, the aroma of freshly roasted beans tantalized my senses, reminding me of life's simple pleasures. In Santiago, I marveled at vibrant textiles handwoven by Tz'utujil women, each piece a testament to their rich cultural heritage.

In San Marcos La Laguna, I met Adelmo. His expressive eyes and weathered face told a story of a life deeply connected to the land. Adelmo's native language was Kaqchikel, an indigenous language deeply rooted in the traditions and culture of the region. Despite the language barrier, we communicated in patchy Spanish, our laughter bridging the gaps.

Adelmo invited me to dinner at his home. I was hesitant, but his genuine warmth eased my fears. Isabela, his wife, greeted me with a smile that radiated kindness. Their children, full of energy and imagination, transformed simple objects into sources of joy. They played with a lemon, using it first as a ball and then pretending it was a rocket ship. Adelmo's home was small but alive with his children's laughter.

We gathered around for a humble yet heartwarming meal, and as we shared stories, I realized how much I had in common with Adelmo and his family. Although we lived in different corners of the world, our lives were intertwined by the same threads of hardship and joy. Both our families knew the sting of poverty and the uncertainty it brings, each day a question mark, wondering if we'd have enough to get by. We both experienced the struggle of being outsiders in a land where our mother tongue was a foreign one, every conversation a potential minefield of misunderstandings. But through it all, we held onto our dreams and hopes, fueled by the same grit and determination.

After dinner, Adelmo motioned for me to follow him. With the last rays of the sun casting a soft glow through the windows, he guided me around his home, eager to share not the grandeur but the small treasures that held the essence of his family's life. Each item he pointed to seemed to carry a story, a memory, or a piece of tradition that he cherished deeply.

As I looked around, I realized that I had, in fact, packed more clothes in my suitcase than this entire Guatemalan family possessed. A wave of shame and guilt washed over me, realizing my overpacking wasn't just about being prepared—it reflected deeper insecurities, my misguided attempt to find security in stuff. The baggage I carried wasn't just physical; it was metaphorical, cluttering my life with things that could never fill the void inside me.

Back home, I lived in a three-bedroom, two-bathroom house, all by myself. Despite the space and all the comforts, the loneliness was palpable. Each room echoed, a reminder of the emptiness and aching loneliness that filled my days. In contrast, Adelmo owned so little, with a small home that barely had enough space for his family, yet it overflowed with warmth and love. Every corner of his home buzzed with life and laughter. In that moment, it was clear: Adelmo, with his modest means and abundant love, was by far, the richer person.

The true richness of life is found in love and connection, and Adelmo embodied this truth in the way he offered kindness to a stranger and in the loving way his family welcomed me, with open arms and open hearts. I learned about love in a whole new way. I always thought the greatest love was the kind you find in fairytales—the kind between princes and princesses. But love is something greater. It's in the way you open your heart and home to someone you just met. It's in the selflessness, the generosity, and the genuine warmth of human connection.

When it was time to leave Guatemala, I battled my behemoth suitcase once more. Realizing it was too burdensome to carry, I let go of my attachment to all the unnecessary things I had packed. I pushed the suitcase over the edge and watched it tumble down the volcano, bouncing and rolling, crashing through bushes and scattering leaves. Each thud and scrape seemed to echo the release of my own burdens.

At the bottom of the volcano, I picked up my battered suitcase, now marked with the journey it had taken. At the airport, security inspected it with confusion, puzzled by its condition. "Don't worry," I told them, "That's just tree sap."

As the plane took off, I watched Guatemala fade into the distance beneath me. The mountains and the lake became smaller, but the lessons I'd learned burned bright.

I knew it was time to find the truths about life they don't teach you in college, the wisdom you can't learn from textbooks. It was time to let the world be my classroom and discover what it truly meant to live.

Chapter 5
Monks, Elephants, and Ping Pong Balls

I arrived in Thailand with a lighter suitcase and a fuller heart. Guatemala taught me lessons, but Thailand was a new dance, a rhythm of tropical islands and bustling cities intertwined with ancient temples and a spiritual harmony that felt timeless.

In Chiang Mai, the streets were alive with color, from bustling markets to ancient temples nestled amidst lush mountains. The temples were more than mere buildings; they were portals to history, stories etched in stone that spoke of devotion, faith, and the search for inner peace. Walking through their sacred grounds, I felt serenity enveloping me like a warm blanket. The air was thick with the scent of incense, and the chants of monks echoed through the hallowed space.

Among the ancient stones and timeless rituals, I found a spot to meditate. Sitting on a cushion softened by years of seekers like me, I crossed my legs and shut my eyes, chasing after inner peace. The solemnity of the temple enveloped me, carrying me upon the distant whispers of monks' chants. Despite the calm around me, my mind was restless.

I struggled to quiet the mental chatter. The more I tried, the more my mind resisted, stubbornly holding onto the past and dreading the uncertainties of the future. My thoughts raced like a wildfire, fueled by regrets and what-ifs, anxieties and fears. Every attempt to focus on my breath was met with a barrage of memories and worries, a relentless storm that refused to calm. I replayed past mistakes like a bad movie stuck on repeat, each scene a reminder of what I could've done differently. And ahead of me, the future loomed like a dense fog, full of unknowns that left me paralyzed, each breath adding fuel to a fire I couldn't control. My mind held tight to the familiar pain of my insecurities, preferring the known discomfort to the risk of letting go. It was like wrestling with a shadow, an elusive opponent that grew stronger the harder I fought. Tears threatened to spill, but I held them back, letting the monks' chants wash over me.

Finally, with a sigh of defeat, I rose from my seat and wandered into the temple's courtyard, tracing my fingers along the ancient stones and intricate carvings. As I wandered through the gardens, I stumbled upon a monk, his orange robes fluttering as he walked toward me.

"Are you enjoying the temple?" he asked.

"It's beautiful," I admitted, "but I can't meditate. I couldn't find my piece of inner peace."

He chuckled, "Have you ever heard about the lotus?" He pointed to the blossoming flower carved in the wall. "The lotus blooms in muddy water, just like inner peace blooms from a messy mind."

I nodded, intrigued.

"Every bit of stillness brings you closer. All you have to do is be with the mud."

...

Leaving the temple with the monk's wisdom still humming in my thoughts, I headed to an elephant sanctuary, where I would be volunteering. Elephants of all ages roamed free, happily grazing through the lush sanctuary.

Many of these elephants had endured years of hardship. Forced into grueling labor in the logging industry and exploited in the tourist trade, they had known nothing but abuse and cruelty. But here, at the sanctuary, they were given a second chance—a shot at freedom and kindness after a life of suffering.

As I fed them bananas and sugar cane, their trunks wrapping around the treats with surprising gentleness, I ran my hands over their scars. These massive creatures, with their rough, wrinkled skin and wise, soulful eyes, carried the weight of their past with quiet dignity.

Their scars mirrored my own wounds I had tried to conceal beneath layers of striving for perfection. Standing among the elephants, I realized my attempts to bury my pain had only deepened its hold.

Elephants are known for having memories like steel traps. Yet these great beasts found a way to live with their wounds. My own wound still ached, surfacing like shadows during what felt like a failed meditation at the temple. Instead of finding peace, I found my pain, raw and unfiltered. Yet here, in the sanctuary, these wise giants taught me a different lesson—they openly carried their scars with grace.

Standing ankle-deep in mud with the elephants, I realized that my attempt to meditate wasn't a failure after all. It was a revelation of the shadows stirring from deep withing me, calling me to embrace the healing I had evaded for too long. This probably wasn't what the monk had in mind when he talked about being with the mud, but there I was, finding answers and a glimpse of peace.

...

My final night in Thailand took me deep into the heart of Bangkok's buzzing streets. Neon lights illuminated every corner, mingling with the tantalizing aromas of street vendors crafting savory Thai dishes that beckoned me further. Traditional music set a rhythmic backdrop for street performers, their dances telling stories amidst the vibrant chaos, while tuk-tuks weaved through narrow alleys, adding to the city's lively pulse.

Among the bustling markets, a man, cloaked in the shadows of a narrow alleyway, approached me with an intriguing invitation.

"Do you want to see a special show? It's free," he said.

Who doesn't love free stuff? Curiosity took the wheel, leading me down dimly lit alleys and up creaking stairs. What awaited was a spectacle unlike any other—naked women performing unexpected feats with ping pong balls, cigarettes, and balloons in between their legs. Half-naked women approached me, offering bottles of alcohol which I politely declined.

What started as an unexpected detour quickly took a turn for the worse. The few tourists watching the show argued loudly with the servers. With my discomfort escalating, I walked swiftly toward the exit. At the door, a man blocked my way, demanding payment for drinks that I didn't even touch. Tensions escalated quickly, and when I threatened to call the police, their own "police" appeared—stern, sharply dressed men, a stark contrast to Thailand's usual warmth.

Adrenaline surged through me as I bolted out the door, their shouts echoing behind me. My heart pounded in my chest as I flew down the narrow staircase, taking the steps two at a time, my mind racing faster than my feet.

Bursting onto the busy streets of Bangkok, I was met with a wall of noise and motion. The market was alive with the shouts of vendors trying to lure tourists, motorbikes weaving through the crowd, and the scent of street food mingling with the humid air. I ducked and weaved through the throng of people, glancing over my shoulder to see the sharply dressed men closing in.

Every turn felt like a gamble, every alley a potential trap. I pushed through a group of tourists, their confused faces a blur as I sprinted past. Spotting a taxi at the curb, I dashed toward it, ignoring the driver's startled expression as I threw myself into the backseat. Relief washed over me as the taxi sped away, the chaos fading in the rearview mirror.

As the city slipped away, my fear morphed into laughter. I had always walked the straight and narrow, tiptoeing through life, scared to death of making mistakes, plotting every move to dodge any missteps. But in doing so, I also dodged the thrill. My life, neat and tidy, missed the spark that lights up when you leap into the unknown, push the envelope, and test the waters. Racing through the streets of Bangkok, I had an epiphany. In my relentless chase for perfection, I'd let spontaneity and adventure slip through my fingers. I had been so afraid to stumble that I had never truly run.

Right then and there, sitting in the taxi, my heart pounding, drenched in sweat, with my hair tousled and wild from the rush, I made a promise to myself. I vowed to break free from the shackles of my own making, to stretch my comfort zone and flirt with the unknown—as long as it didn't involve naked women and ping-pong balls.

Chapter 6
Dolphins and Drug Dealers

San Pedro, Belize welcomed me like an old friend with its warm, sea-scented breezes and the soothing murmur of Caribbean waves. It was here, on this island known for its barrier reefs and aquatic wonders that I aimed to dive into the unknown, both beneath the sea and within myself.

The ocean had always been a symbol of my deepest fears. Since that summer day at four years old when I was raped at daycare after a swimming lesson, water had turned from a life-giving essence into a haunting reminder of my darkest moments. At eighteen, I took the plunge to learn the basics of swimming, but my relationship with water was still tangled in fear. Now, in San Pedro, I was on the edge of a personal reckoning, ready to face my enduring fear by learning how to scuba dive.

My instructor, Jason, was born and raised on this island, possessing a bond with the ocean that ran as deep as the coral reefs. To him, the sea was home, a place of comfort and familiarity. But for me, it was a constant reminder of my darkest fears and buried traumas. Where he saw freedom and adventure, I saw the ghosts of my past lurking beneath the waves.

We started with books and lectures—a litany of the hazards of scuba diving, each one seemingly crafted to amplify my dread. Then came the pool sessions. In that controlled environment, my anxiety hit new heights, but I managed to keep it in check, learning to breathe through the regulator, clear my mask, and communicate underwater.

But when we transitioned to the open ocean, my panic surged with every wave. The warm waters, which should have been comforting, instead stirred a primal terror. I felt unsafe and utterly out of control—emotions I hadn't allowed myself to feel since I was four years old. With each swell, memories I'd long suppressed found their way to the surface. The vulnerability, the helplessness, the sense of being at the mercy of something far greater than myself—it all came flooding back. My fear culminated in a distressing yet all-too-human reaction: I vomited, my fear and breakfast spilling out, some of it, unfortunately, on Jason.

Humiliated, defeated, and gasping for breath, I floated on the ocean's surface, the salty mix of sea and bile lingering in my mouth.

"Hey, it's okay," Jason reassured me, his voice a calm anchor in the chaos.

"I can't do this. It's too much," I admitted, shame coloring my words.

With a patient smile and understanding eyes, Jason helped me tidy up and readjust my scuba gear. "The ocean won't drown you," he said softly. "But the fear will."

Jason extended his hand to me, an unspoken invitation to trust not just him but the sea itself. I clasped his hand, our fingers locking in a silent pact between teacher and student. Together, we dove beneath the waves, leaving my fears behind as we ventured deeper into the heart of the ocean.

Beneath the surface, the ocean unfurled its vibrant splendor. Schools of multicolored fish flitted among the coral, their scales glinting like jewels in the dappled sunlight reaching into the depths. The coral reefs were a living kaleidoscope, waving gently in the current. Sea turtles, with their mottled green and brown shells, moved with effortless grace, a perfect contrast to the sleek, gray bodies of nurse sharks roaming the ocean floor below. Alive with color and life, the majesty of the sea washed away my lingering fear as my breath fell into rhythm with the gentle flow of the water.

Day after day, as the sun rose over San Pedro, I donned my scuba gear, each time a little more deftly than the last. With every dive, my plunge into the ocean's heart became less of a confrontation and more of a communion. The fear, though always there, started to fade, becoming a familiar companion rather than an overwhelming adversary.

I grew bolder with each dive, venturing further to witness the marvels of the deep. What once was a monolith of my fears began to unfold as a playground ripe for exploration. I encountered wonders I had only ever seen through the glass walls of aquariums: vivid coral reefs teeming with life, playful pods of dolphins dancing through the waves, secretive nooks where shy creatures lurked, and open waters where schools of fish shimmered like living constellations.

Despite the fear tingling in my veins with each dive, I learned how to calm it, using the rhythm of the ocean and the cadence of my own breath as my guide. The ocean taught me that fear wasn't my adversary; it was my teacher. Fear showed me the parts of myself that still needed nurturing, the areas where I was still raw and unfinished. It wasn't there to break me but to shape me, to reveal where I needed to grow. Fear wasn't a barrier but a bridge, guiding me toward understanding and embracing the depths of my true self.

...

On land, San Pedro's charm was irresistible. The island's rhythm was a gentle, steady beat. My search for the island's best sunset brought me to a secluded pier on the western coast. Stretching out into the shimmering turquoise waters, its weathered wooden planks bleached by countless sunsets. Seagulls circled overhead, their cries blending with the soft lapping of waves against the wooden posts.

It was there that I met two men whose rugged looks told tales of their own. Their skin was a living canvas, each tattoo a chapter from their hard-lived stories. Intricate designs snaking across their forearms, symbols and scripts intertwined in shades of black and gray.

The taller one, arms crossed, gave me a once-over with a mix of curiosity and suspicion. "You here for the good weed?" he asked, his voice rough.

I shook my head. "Nope, just here to watch the sunset."

There was a pause, the ocean's whisper the only sound between us. Then, they burst into laughter, a deep, rumbling sound.

"The sunset, huh?" the other man said, his tattoos crinkling as he grinned. "You're a long way from the tourist spots just for a sunset."

They moved aside, making space on the pier's weathered boards. "Well then, have a seat," the taller man said, a hint of warmth breaking through his tough exterior.

The wooden planks creaked as we settled down. Watching the sunset, I shared stories of my scuba diving adventures, tales of facing my fears and finding hope. My words seemed to strike a chord, bridging the gap between our worlds.

The man with the weathered face leaned toward me, his eyes brimming with untold stories. "Hope," he said thoughtfully, "kept me alive. They locked me up for a crime I didn't commit. Took 'em seven years to realize I was innocent and let me go."

I sat there, silent, my gaze locked on his. His eyes had seen the bleakness of a prison cell while never losing sight of freedom, with his son waiting for him beyond the bars that confined him. It was this vision, this unwavering hope, that etched such depth and resilience into his gaze. His eyes didn't just reflect a soul that had endured; they shone with the light of a spirit that had refused to be extinguished.

"There were days, so many damn days, when I wanted to die, when the weight of those walls seemed too heavy." He paused, gathering himself. "But hope... hope's got roots that go deep, even in jail. And poetry," he smiled, a flicker of light breaking through, "Poetry kept the hope alive, kept me alive."

"Could you share some of your poetry?" I asked, my voice a mixture of reverence and curiosity.

His smile broadened, and with a nod that seemed to acknowledge the sacredness of the exchange, he began to recite. His voice carried a rhythm like the waves hitting the shore. His words wove a tapestry as rich and vivid as the sunset before us, each line a thread in the fabric of his reclaimed life.

As he recited, the world seemed still—his voice was the only thing anchoring us to that moment. In the space between his lines, I saw the truth in his eyes and the strength in his stance. Behind the rugged tattoos and the hardened façade, hope and love pulsed in his veins.

Despite the vastly different paths, his poetry became a bridge connecting his world to mine. There, on a humble pier, as our stories unfurled alongside the ebbing daylight, we transformed from strangers to the most unlikely of friends.

What do a lawyer and a drug dealer have in common? Turns out, everything. Both of us had seen the dark side of life, faced our own demons, and come out the other side with hope still flickering within us. We knew the taste of fear, the sting of betrayal, and the bittersweet flavor of redemption. We had both danced with danger, walked the tightrope between survival and surrender, and emerged stronger for it.

He had his hustle, and I had mine. Different stages, same play. We both knew what it meant to fight for a better life, to push against the odds, and to hold onto our dreams when the world seemed determined to crush them.

As they inhaled their last breaths of weed and I soaked in the last flickers of sunlight, we weren't just people from different worlds. We were kindred spirits, bound by our shared experiences, our struggles, and our victories.

Chapter 7
Sensations

As the morning light broke, the melodic sound of Muslim prayers echoed through the streets of Marrakech, Morocco. On my first morning in Marrakech, I rose from bed faced with what I thought would be a straightforward task: withdrawing cash from an ATM. But as I made my way to the ATM, I discovered that every machine in the city would only take a four-digit PIN: mine was seven.

Marrakech, also known as Marra-cash, was notorious for only accepting cash. Exhausted from scouring the city for an ATM and dehydrated from my inability to buy water to battle the heat of the African summer sun, I gave up searching for the ATM, realizing that I could send myself money through a wire transfer.

Frustration mounting, I reached the wire transfer office only to be told that my driver's license wasn't good enough. They needed my passport. I trudged back to where I was staying, the heat unyielding, my patience wearing thin.

On my way back, passport in hand, I crossed paths with two young Moroccan boys. They were skinny, fragile like saplings in a desert. One of the boys stepped closer and said, "You're going the wrong way. The market is the other way."

I paused to thank him for his helpfulness and to explain that I wasn't heading to the market. My words were cut short as I noticed the other boy stealthily trying to slip his hand into my bag.

Reacting instinctively, with years of Muay Thai and Jiu-Jitsu under my belt, I turned to face the boy trying to snatch my bag. In one fluid motion, my elbow found its mark on his face. The sudden impact startled him, making him stagger back and let out a shriek. Both boys, realizing they were in over their heads, took off running.

Shaken but unharmed, I continued my way to the wire transfer office. After taking out enough cash to keep me afloat in Morocco for a few weeks, I headed back out to find my way back to where I was staying.

Then, as if on cue, another pair of young boys approached. One of them started, "You're going the wrong way. The market is…" But before he could finish, I spotted his partner behind me, his hand creeping toward my bag. Instinctively, I leaned back, pinning the would-be thief against the wall. The collision sent him stumbling to the ground. After scrambling to his feet, the boys ran off.

Overwhelmed by fear and exhaustion, I had a sinking realization that I was lost. The winding streets of Marrakech were an unsolvable maze. The dusty, uneven paths kicked up clouds with every hurried step, coating my shoes and clothes in a fine layer of grit. I wanted to cry, feeling utterly alone as I scrambled through alleys, turning back whenever I hit a dead end or the buildings looked too unfamiliar. Every shadow seemed threatening, and the vibrant chaos of the city felt more like a trap than an adventure. The air was thick with the scent of spices and the distant hum of the market, but in my disoriented state, it all seemed to close in around me, amplifying my sense of isolation and fear.

A man approached me. "Are you lost?" he asked gently.

My heart pounded in my chest, mistrust and fear gnawing at me. After my morning encounters, I didn't know if I could trust anyone. I didn't answer, just quickened my pace, every instinct telling me to keep my distance.

"I think I know where you're staying. I saw you walking this morning," he continued, but his words only heightened my anxiety. "I'm trying to help you. I don't want your money. I just want to help," he insisted.

Still unsure and wary, I listened as he offered, "I'll walk on the other side of the street from you, okay? I'll walk you home. Just follow me."

Hesitantly, I followed, my eyes never leaving him. Slowly, the doors of the buildings, each with their unique designs and vibrant colors, started to look familiar. The beautiful doors of Marrakech, so varied and intricate, became beacons guiding me home.

As we walked, the man started sharing his wisdom about the city. "Marrakech isn't a place to navigate with a map on your phone. Look around. Look at the doors. Look at the mosque towers. What do you smell? What do you hear? This is how you find your way," he explained, his voice calm and steady.

He explained how the shadows of the mosques shifted during the day, offering clues to direction. "The noise of the crows will lead you to the market. If you smell spices, you're near your home," he said. "But if you catch the stink of the tannery, you're walking deeper into the market and away from home."

Throughout our walk, he continued to detail the various sensory cues of Marrakech's streets until we arrived at the familiar green door of where I was staying.

Grateful for his help, I reached into my bag and offered him some money as a token of my appreciation. He gently waved it away, refusing to accept it. "Best of luck, my friend," he said with a warm smile before parting ways.

Exhausted and still trembling from the morning's ordeals, I lay in bed, trying to process the whirlwind of events that had unfolded in just a few hours on my first morning in Marrakech. As the adrenaline wore off, tears welled in my eyes. Fear still clung to my bones, and a part of me yearned to leave this city that had so quickly pushed me to my limits.

But as I lay there, the sounds of life bustling outside my window seemed to call out, inviting me to embrace the unfamiliar. This morning had been a wild initiation—a brush with danger that left me unharmed but afraid. I ruminated in my fear, but remembering the kindness of the stranger who steered me back without expecting anything in return helped me navigate through my fear. Something deep within me whispered to stay, face the fear, and find my way in Marrakech.

In the following days, I mastered the art of navigating Marrakech's medinas and markets. I relied on my senses, tuning in to the city's unique symphony. The rich, aromatic spices in the air guided me, the chatter of vendors and the clinking of pottery became auditory beacons, and the vibrant doors, each with their own color and pattern, served as markers on my mental map.

I watched the shadows stretch and dance, cast by the towering minarets of Marrakech's mosques. They became my natural sundials, guiding my way. With an internal map forming, I found a new rhythm, syncing with the five calls to prayer that echoed through the streets, each call a marker of time and a heartbeat, connecting me to the soul of the city.

With a welcome heart, I leaned into the experience, not just observing but engaging. I struck up conversations with shopkeepers in the bustling souks, learning the art of haggling and the stories behind their crafts. Over cups of mint tea, I shared laughs and tales with locals, bridging the gap between our worlds, their warmth and openness as intoxicating as the city itself.

I was invited into their homes, where I savored home-cooked tagines and exchanged more than just pleasantries: we shared dreams and perspectives, gaining an understanding of each other's worlds. I learned to cook with them, dance with them, and even join in their traditions and celebrations. Every interaction, every shared meal, drew me closer to the heart of Marrakesh. I wasn't just passing through—I was becoming a part of the fabric woven into the everyday life of the city.

Even though I traveled to Marrakesh heartbroken and alone, I discovered a whole new kind of love. Love was in the symphony of sounds that filled the air—the melodic call to prayer, the vibrant chatter of the souks, and the soulful strumming of a street musician's oud. It was in the intoxicating smells of spices wafting through the market, the scent of freshly baked bread, and the fragrant allure of jasmine in the evening breeze.

I fell in love with new experiences, each one a brushstroke, painting a vivid picture of life in Marrakesh, from navigating the labyrinthine streets to savoring the rich flavors of a perfectly spiced tagine, every moment an adventure, a story waiting to be told.

Here, I discovered the love of strangers, who greeted me with warm smiles and open hearts. They shared their wisdom, their traditions, and their stories, teaching me that love lives in the simple, everyday gestures—a shared laugh, a helping hand, a moment of understanding.

After leaving a failed relationship and feeling lost in the search for love, I realized that love isn't something to be found; it's something that exists all around us—we simply need to open our eyes, our hearts, and our senses to feel it.

Chapter 8
Flamenco and Fire

Seville pulsed with life and history in the South of Spain, with its cobblestone streets winding through old Moorish architecture, vibrant plazas filled with the scent of orange blossoms, and a grand cathedral that seemed to touch the sky. The city came alive with the sounds of horse-drawn carriages clattering along, street musicians strumming their guitars, and the distant toll of church bells. Seville was more than a place, it was a feeling: a warm, inviting embrace of culture and tradition that wraps around you the moment you step into its heart.

In Seville, I threw myself into learning flamenco, a dance that felt like an art form that seemed to breathe the very soul of the city. At first, I felt awkward and out of place, my movements stiff and uncertain. Flamenco was an unmastered language, full of fire and flair, that I couldn't quite grasp.

As the steps and movements became more familiar, I headed to a street plaza where the locals gathered in the evenings to dance flamenco. The street was electrifying, and the locals moved with effortless grace, their bodies telling tales and sharing emotions that words could never express. They weren't just dancing; they were living and breathing the music, their movements a seamless flow of expression.

As I stood at the edge of the crowd, feeling out of place, a man emerged from the sea of dancers. He was the quintessential tall, dark, and handsome Spaniard, his presence commanding yet inviting. He extended his hand to me, a silent invitation to join the dance. With a touch of hesitation, I accepted, and he gently led me into the heart of the crowd. As we began to move, my steps were awkward and mechanical, each one a reflection of the calculated moves I had learned over the past week.

He sensed my hesitation and leaned in, whispering, "Don't think. Feel."

Slowly, I began to let go. I started to feel—the warmth of the air around us and between us, the symphony of scents in the plaza, from the saffron-infused paella and tapas to the distinct smell of him close to me. Music and laughter filled the air, blending with the rhythm of clapping hands and dancing feet.

The more I felt, the less I thought. My mind, perpetually shadowed by the sadness of the past, doubts of the present, and worries of the future, began to quiet. As my thoughts dissolved into the night air, I was able to simply feel.

My steps, though still imperfect, carried a newfound vitality. Each movement breathed life into my soul. My feet tapped rhythmically against the ground. My arms moved with grace and passion. My body swayed with the intense, fiery spirit of flamenco, every gesture infused with raw, uncontainable energy.

Beside me, the Spaniard, with his piercing, dark-brown eyes, matched my every move. His presence was magnetic, his movements a masterful blend of power and elegance as his feet struck the ground with decisive authority, echoing the deep, primal beats of the music. His arms, strong and fluid, danced through the air, leading and responding in a dance of unspoken dialogue.

Together, we moved under the starlit sky, our bodies in perfect harmony. Every step, every turn, every spirited clap of his hands and graceful twirl of my skirt filled the night with an intoxicating sense of life. Time ceased to exist as we lost ourselves in the dance, each breath, each beat, each laugh infusing us with pure, unadulterated joy. It was more than dancing; it was the sheer exhilaration of being alive.

From Seville, I made my way to Barcelona, a city where history and modernity waltz together like old friends. The streets unfolded like a living canvas, a mosaic of Gothic charm interwoven with a modern flair.

My last night in Barcelona coincided with the Festival of Sant Joan, a traditional celebration marking the summer solstice. Massive bonfires lit every street, honoring the sun that could burn away sins and misfortunes. Locals and travelers alike gathered, dancing and leaping over the flames, leaving the past behind and jumping into a hopeful future.

Swept away in the Festival of Sant Joan, I danced with locals and fellow travelers as the night sky exploded with fireworks. Music and singing filled the air, and the rhythm of dancing feet seemed to sync with my own heartbeat.

Locals handed me furniture to throw into the fire, a symbolic act of burning what weighs down the soul. Every item I tossed into the flames felt like letting go of a piece of my past, the smoke taking away old worries and fears.

Through the roaring flames, a firecracker tossed into the fire by one of the children zipped through the air in a wild, unpredictable arc, flying inches from my face. The sharp scent of burning suddenly filled the air. I realized that the fire had burned some of my hair.

Normally, I rigidly gravitated toward order and predictability, finding peace in well-laid plans and a sense of control. Yet here I was, amid chaos, flames dancing wildly, the air electric with excitement and uncertainty. What I lacked in control, I gained in freedom. I stood in the center of chaos, and I was okay. More than okay—I was vividly alive.

Chapter 9
The Shit and the Shaman

With a backpack as my trusty companion, I set off to Peru. In Paracas, penguins danced by the shore, and in Huacachina, the towering sand dunes called me to adventure. The geoglyphs of Nazca unfolded beneath me, ancient and enigmatic. I watched condors soar majestically over the Colca Canyon and joined miners in Arequipa, carving the volcanic white stone that built the "White City." The villages along Lake Titicaca whispered tales of simple, timeless living. The ruins of Machu Picchu and the winding Inca Trail left me spellbound, each step resonating with history. Peru, in all its splendor, left me in awe.

I found refuge in Cusco, the once-glorious heart of the Inca Empire. Its streets were adorned with ancient Inca walls, colonial balconies, and vibrant markets bustling with life. However, the elevation and steep streets of the Andes proved too challenging for my body to endure.

At first, the symptoms of altitude sickness whispered their arrival—a mild headache and a hint of shortness of breath as I hiked through the Andes. But as the days wore on, those whispers grew into a deafening roar. One early morning, while searching for the perfect spot to watch the sunrise, my stomach turned traitor, churning violently.

In a state of panic, I stumbled through the steep streets, desperately trying to find my way back to some semblance of safety. Disoriented and ill, I hit my breaking point. With no other options, I dropped my pants and crouched right there on the street. My embarrassment peaked when I realized that I had just pooped on a street corner under a shrine of the Virgin Mary. I thought to myself, *Well, if there is a hell, this is probably my ticket.*

Lost and bewildered, I found myself drifting on a secluded street far from the center of Cusco, which seemed to exist in a world of its own. The walls of the shops and homes were painted with symbols and images of the mountains and creatures I'd encountered throughout Peru. Intrigued, I glanced through shop windows and saw an array of mystical items: vibrant plants, shimmering crystals, and bottles filled with potions.

As I continued down the mysterious street, one window pulled me in. Flickering candles inside the home cast a warm, inviting glow, drawing me in like a moth to a flame. I walked closer to the window and the glow that seemed to whisper my name. My trance was abruptly broken as the door suddenly creaked open.

There she was: Ayar, an older woman who called herself a shaman. Her face, etched with lines of wisdom and experience, told stories without words. Ayar wore a dress with brightly woven patterns, talismans hanging around her neck, her long, silver hair flowing freely, framing her face with dignified grace.

Ayar looked at me with a smile and said, "Welcome back, old friend."

I was confused. I had never met her before. She was so distinct, so unforgettable, that I was certain I had never seen her before. But there it was, plain as day, a moment that felt like destiny had been waiting for me to catch up.

Bewildered, I stared at her silently as if I had lost the ability to speak. Ayar extended her hand, and with a gentle nod, welcomed me inside. I followed her, as if pulled by an unseen force. She offered me a seat by a warm fire and handed me a cup of tea.

"What name do they call you?" she asked softly.

I stammered, feeling as if I had forgotten my own name. The words caught in my throat before I finally managed to respond, "Lani."

Ayar's smile deepened. "We go by many names," she said softly.

"I don't," I replied, shaking my head. "My name is so short; I've never had a nickname."

Ayar chuckled, a warm, melodic sound that seemed to resonate with the flickering flames. "Ah, Lani, sometimes the shortest names carry the greatest weight." She paused, then asked, "What does your name mean?"

"It's Hawaiian," I explained. "It means heaven, sky, or the beyond."

Ayar's eyes sparkled with recognition. "Heaven, sky, the beyond... Lani. A bridge between worlds. It suits you," she smiled.

I was too fascinated with the objects around her home to worry about how she seemed to speak in riddles. Ayar noticed my wide-eyed curiosity as I took in the surroundings. As my gaze locked onto a large crystal, Ayar caught my stare, a knowing smile playing on her lips.

She returned with a purple pouch filled with various stones, her eyes sparkling with a secret she wished to share.

"Go ahead," she said, holding the pouch open. "Pick one."

As I reached into the pouch, my fingers were immediately drawn to a large, blue stone, marbled with waves of white and black, like a miniature, turbulent ocean captured within. Feeling the cool, heavy weight of the stone in my hand, the colors shifted subtly under the candlelight, almost as if it was alive.

Ayar nodded, her smile deepening. "Good choice," she murmured. "That stone has a story to tell. *You* have a story to tell.'" She looked at me with knowing eyes and said, "Hold the stone, close your eyes, and breathe into it. Breathe life into it."

I hesitated for a moment. She was a complete stranger, yet somehow, I felt complete trust. I held the stone tightly in my hand, closed my eyes, and took a deep breath. As I exhaled, I blew gently into the stone, opened my eyes, and handed it back to Ayar. She took it carefully, cradling it in her weathered hands. Holding it tightly, Ayar closed her eyes, and murmured words I couldn't understand. Her voice was soft, melodic, and the air around us seemed to hum. She appeared to be in a trance, communicating with the stone or perhaps something beyond.

After a moment that felt like an eternity, Ayar finally opened her eyes and looked at me intently.

"You're seeking, searching for something bigger than you know. There's more out there than your eyes can see. There's more."

She paused, allowing the words to sink in. "You are on a journey," she spoke softly, "But you must throw away the map. Even with it, you find yourself lost. This is your compass," Ayar said, tapping the space between my eyebrows. "This is your compass," she said, gently placing her hand on my heart. "This is your compass," she said, pointing to my stomach.

Ayar took my hand, guiding me to stand. She then started moving around me in circles, every so often brushing and batting me with a bundle of leaves. She chanted words, tumbling out in a rhythm I couldn't decipher, but one word stood out, striking me like a lightning bolt. *Bruja.*

Her voice rose and fell with the cadence of her chants, like waves crashing against the shore. The word *bruja* echoed in my mind, sharp and stinging. Witch. Sorceress.

When I was a child, I could smell the rain before it fell, the scent of damp earth filling my senses. I would dance, calling the rain, and the skies would answer. I felt the emotions of others as they entered a room, their feelings swirling around me like an invisible mist.

My dreams were vivid tapestries of scent and taste, so intense that I would wake with a nosebleed. And those dreams wove themselves into reality. I finished people's sentences, fragments remembered from my dreams.

I learned the flavors of emotions long before understanding their depths. Anger tasted like battery acid, burning and harsh. Shame tasted like sour milk, curdled and bitter.

I had an imaginary friend, like many children do. Mine was Carolina, who I later discovered was my grandmother who passed away shortly after my father's birth. Some people found me odd. Some people were afraid of me. I could taste their fear like heat on my tongue. They called me *bruja*—witch. A name I loathed.

One day, I wrote *bruja* on a piece of paper and drew a black box over it, concealing it from sight. I buried it deep in the dirt and covered it with twigs and leaves. From that moment, the vivid sensations faded, blending into the ordinary. Sometimes, I felt a flicker, a whisper, but I easily brushed it aside.

But now, with Ayar chanting, the word *bruja* reverberating in the air, I felt my blood boiling. My mouth filled with the acrid taste of battery acid and sour milk. Ayar continued to move around me, circling, brushing me with leaves, her chants a haunting melody. She tapped my shoulders and back, each a rhythmic beat, until she suddenly slapped my back. I coughed, and the bitter taste vanished.

Ayar's voice grew louder. Her words were heavy with the weight of the past, each syllable laden with memories I had fought to bury. She painted a vivid picture, describing through my eyes my eighth birthday when my grandfather decided to take his own life.

As she spoke, her words encircling me like a tightening noose, I felt a surge of rage rise within me, the sour taste of shame coating my tongue. I felt violated and exposed, as if she had torn open an old wound and laid my pain bare. My hands clenched into fists. My anger flared, burning hotter with each word she uttered as she unraveled the secrets I hid closely in my heart.

Ayar's chanting grew softer and more soothing, as if she were singing a lullaby to my wounded soul. She looked at me with wise, ancient eyes, her gaze penetrating and compassionate.

"Your pain is not meant to be carried alone," she whispered.

Suddenly, Ayar placed a liquid in her mouth. Without warning, she spat it onto me. The shock of it took my breath away. And just as quickly as she spat, the pain left me, draining out of my legs and into the ground. The sensation was startling, like a bolt of lightning grounding through my body, pulling the anguish and despair away, leaving me light and unburdened.

Ayar shook her bundle of leaves rhythmically, as if sweeping away unseen shadows from my body.

"Why are you here?" she asked, her voice firm yet gentle.

"I got lost this morning," I replied, my voice uncertain.

"Why are you here?" she repeated, still brushing me with the leaves.

"I'm traveling through Peru," I said, the words feeling inadequate.

"Why are you here?" she asked again, her tone growing more insistent.

"I'm taking time off of work because my life feels empty, and I don't know how to make it whole," I admitted, feeling a pang of vulnerability.

"Why are you here?" she demanded sharply, her eyes piercing into mine.

"Because I was called," I spat out, my voice matching her intensity. I was startled by my own words, embarrassed by the force with which I had shouted. Ayar stopped circling and stood in front of me, a proud smile playing on her lips. She cupped my face in her hands, her gaze deep and knowing.

"Whenever you feel lost, remember that you were called. Remember," Ayar said, each syllable echoing in my mind, sending ripples throughout every fiber and cell of my body.

Ayar guided me to a seat by the fire, her movements gentle and reassuring.

"How about we eat?" she suggested as she moved into the kitchen. While she prepared the food, I wandered around her home, drawn to the items that caught my eye earlier that morning.

From the kitchen, Ayar called out, "What if these objects had stories? What if they could speak? What would they say?"

I picked up each item, one by one, and allowed my imagination to take flight. Like a child lost in a game of make-believe, I imagined and narrated the stories they might tell. An old, worn-out book whispered tales of distant lands and adventures long past. A delicate, hand-painted vase spoke of love and loss, its intricate patterns echoing the emotions of those who had once cherished it. Every object held a fragment of history, a whisper of a memory.

When Ayar returned from the kitchen, her face was streaked with tears. She stood silently, her eyes overflowing with emotion. With each object and each story, I had unknowingly touched on memories and loved ones that seemed lost to her. As I told their stories aloud, I was breathing life into forgotten fragments of the past. The room felt alive with the presence of the past. It was as if the very walls were listening, absorbing the stories and holding them close, promising that they would never be forgotten.

After we finished eating, Ayar and I stood by the doorway, the firelight casting warm shadows around us. We hugged, a deep and heartfelt embrace.

"Thank you," I said, my voice soft but sincere.

"Any time in any time," she replied with a gentle smile. "I'll pray for you in your travels. I hope they help you remember. They're waiting for you to remember."

Her words puzzled me, but I tucked them away, knowing they held some significance I had yet to understand. As I walked away,

I kept glancing back at Ayar's home, half-expecting it to vanish like a dream.

As I moved away from Ayar's home, my ears began to ring, a low and distant hum filling the air. The sound was strange and hypnotic, like the resonant vibrations of a singing bowl, deep and steady. It was a quiet yet persistent melody that beckoned me to follow.

Drawn by the sound, I walked slowly, each step guided by the hum that grew slightly louder with every stride. I followed its call, the low tone reverberating through my bones, leading me closer and closer to the center of the city. When the hum reached its loudest, it suddenly ceased, and I found myself standing in front of the home where I was staying—the place where I wished I had actually pooped that morning.

Chapter 10
The Place Where Things Are Made

Tromsø, Norway, a city cloaked in snow and darkness, was located over two hundred miles north of the Arctic Circle. I arrived in January, the time of year with the darkest nights, shortest days, and coldest winters, with one mission: to see the Northern Lights.

I joined a group of travelers from around the world as we made our way to our campsite. We gathered around a fire as we ate a hearty reindeer stew. Among the group was an elderly Welsh couple, whose story was one of love and urgency. The wife, fighting a degenerative eye condition, wished to witness the aurora borealis before her vision faded.

As the night wore on, a ferocious snowstorm erupted, turning the serene snowfall into a wild, untamed force. Visibility quickly vanished as the storm intensified, cloaking the sky in a swirling haze of white. The group hastily retreated to the cars that would take them back into town, their hurried footsteps leaving deep impressions in the snow.

I followed their snowy trail, my breath visible in the frigid air, when suddenly, a sharp ringing filled my ears, morphing into a low, resonant hum that seemed to vibrate through my entire body like an otherworldly summons that I couldn't ignore. Beyond all reason, I knew I needed to stay.

I stopped in my tracks, scanning the campsite. The tour guide looked at me with a mix of concern and frustration. "There's no way you'll see the Northern Lights with this visibility," he said, his voice barely audible over the howling wind. "The storm is only going to get worse."

"I understand," I replied, my resolve unwavering. "But I still want to try."

He raised an eyebrow, clearly puzzled by my determination. "If you stay, you'll be out here alone. Are you sure you want to stay?"

"Yes," I nodded. "It's okay."

He let out a sigh, his breath visible in the frigid air. "Alright, but you'll have to keep the fire going by yourself."

"I can do that," I assured him.

"Have you ever made a fire or kept one going before?" he asked, skepticism creeping into his tone.

"No," I admitted, "but I can figure it out."

He shook his head, the lines on his face deepening with worry. "You can't sleep for more than two hours at a time, or else the fire will die and you'll have to start it again."

"I understand," I said, meeting his gaze. "I'll manage."

Clearly annoyed and eager to get home, he brushed me off with a wave of his hand. "Fine. I'll be back in the morning at ten a.m. to pick you up. Good luck."

"Thank you," I replied, watching as he trudged back to the group, leaving me alone in the swirling snow.

After the last of the group headed out, I settled into my tent. In the center stood a small furnace with a steady fire, its warmth radiating through the space. In one corner was a pile of reindeer-skin blankets and in another a neatly rolled-up sleeping bag. The tent's window, a small, clear, plastic section near the top, offered a glimpse of the outside world, framing the swirling snowstorm.

As I waited for the weather to calm, I shrugged off my jacket and heavy layers, feeling relief from their weight, and made a pot of tea over the small fire, its warmth offering a bit of comfort in the cold. The fire crackled softly, a soothing sound against the howling wind outside. Every now and then, I'd peek out the tent's window, my breath fogging up the small pane as I scanned the sky for any sign of the Northern Lights.

The storm eventually stopped, leaving silence in its wake. The snow-covered world outside glowed faintly under the moonlight, serene and undisturbed. I continued to watch the skies through the window, my eyes straining for any flicker of color, occasionally unzipping the tent door to peek outside. Hours slipped by, the anticipation building, each minute stretching into what felt like an eternity. The night was quiet, almost eerily so, save for the gentle rustle of the tent fabric in the lingering breeze.

Out of nowhere, a flash of green caught my eye through the window. My heart skipped a beat as I bolted outside, the cold air slamming into me like a freight train, its icy grip stealing my breath away. And there it was, the aurora borealis, putting on a show just for me. The Northern Lights unfurled in a mesmerizing dance across the starry sky—bands of green mingling with purples and blues, swirling and twisting like a celestial ballet.

As I ventured further from the tent, the snow got deeper, first reaching my knees, then my waist. It was like wading through an ocean of powder, each step a slow-motion plunge into the white abyss. I didn't mind the snow. I didn't even feel it. I was too captivated, too enamored with the sky above me, the stars glittering like diamonds scattered across a velvet canvas and the glowing aurora painting the sky.

After the lights faded into the night, I trudged back to my tent through the deep snow. Stepping inside, reality hit me. In my excitement to witness the Northern Lights, I had forgotten to wear my waterproof layers. My clothes were soaked, clinging to my skin with a cold that seemed to seep straight into my bones.

With urgency, I peeled off my drenched clothes, laying them out near the furnace in a desperate attempt to dry them. What had been a comforting fire now turned into my lifeline against the freezing night.

Keeping the fire going was a lesson in humility. Every log I tossed in the fire seemed to burn in an instant. The flames sputtered and flickered like a half-hearted promise that couldn't quite deliver. As the night wore on, each moment became a battle against the cold, the frost creeping in like an uninvited guest.

As I scrambled around the tent naked, trying to generate heat, a sharp, acrid smell pierced the air—the scent of burning plastic. To my horror, I saw my polyester blend socks had gotten too close to the furnace and were now smoldering. With my toes numb and freezing, I grabbed my mittens and frantically slipped them onto my feet, hoping they'd provide some makeshift protection against the biting cold. It was a desperate move in a desperate moment.

There I was, naked and freezing, my breath hanging in the air of the tent like tiny ghosts swirling in the dim light. Desperate to fend off the cold, I started doing jumping jacks, running in place, and any other movement that came to mind. But the cold was unrelenting. My joints began to stiffen. My body stopped shivering, and my teeth stopped chattering, but the cold was still there, creeping into my bones.

At first, my mind raced with fear and a flurry of ideas to keep warm. Desperation fueled my thoughts, each one more frantic than the last. But gradually, my thoughts began to slow, like a river freezing over. The adrenaline ebbed away, replaced by a heavy, bone-deep weariness.

I decided to lie next to the fire, hoping its warmth would be enough to keep me alive. Too tired to even consider unrolling a sleeping bag, I grabbed a reindeer skin and huddled beneath it as I lay directly on the tent floor, the hard surface a stark reminder of my precarious situation.

I fought sleep with everything I had, but my mind felt empty, unable to string together a single coherent thought. I lay there, staring at the fire, watching the flames dance and flicker, their light casting shifting shadows on the tent walls.

In an instant, I was no longer staring into the fire. Instead, I found myself hovering above, looking at my motionless body next to the fire. My face, lit by the fire's unsteady glow, was a mask of exhaustion and resignation, eyes open but unblinking and lips slightly parted as if caught between sleep and consciousness. The reindeer skin lay draped over me, barely offering any warmth against the creeping cold. I appeared so small and fragile, a solitary figure in the vast, relentless expanse of the Arctic night.

As I gazed down at my body beneath me, a low, deep hum pierced the silence, echoing from somewhere above. I looked up, trying to pinpoint its source, but all I saw was darkness. The darkness began to close in around me like a thick, impenetrable shroud. It was as if the very fabric of the night had folded in on itself, enveloping me in an abyss.

The darkness consumed everything, making it impossible to tell if I was on Earth, above it, or somewhere in between. There was no horizon, no sense of up or down, just an endless void that seemed to stretch on forever. In the nothingness, I felt no cold, no pain, no fear. I felt nothing.

As I floated in the boundless expanse, a sense of timelessness washed over me. Seconds, minutes, hours—none of it mattered. It was as if I had slipped beyond the grasp of time itself.

Through the abyss, tiny pinpricks of light began to pierce the darkness. They were distant and faint, like stars peeking through a thick fog. As I watched, they grew brighter and more numerous, clustering together to form intricate patterns and constellations. The stars shimmered with a soft, otherworldly glow, blending with vibrant hues of green, purple, and blue, reminiscent of the Northern Lights. The colors swirled and flowed, creating a mesmerizing tapestry of shifting light and color. Each constellation seemed alive, pulsating with energy, casting a radiant glow that illuminated the surrounding void.

They were more than just random patterns. They formed pathways that seemed to stretch endlessly into the abyss, the luminous trails resembling the vines and roots of a tree, moving in every possible direction, intertwining and branching off into the infinite expanse. These constellations twisted and turned, creating a complex network of light that pulsed with life.

In a whisper of thought, I asked, "Where am I?"

Suddenly, pillars of light appeared, towering and radiant. The answer to my question didn't come in words but through images emanating from the pillars of light. I saw the birth and death of stars, the genesis of life, the Garden of Eden, and countless snapshots of existence. It was a visual symphony of the universe's story, from its most grandiose cosmic events to the subtlest nuances of life. I knew exactly where I was. I was nowhere and everywhere. I was in the place where things were made.

From the pillars of light came a question: "Where do you want to go?"

"I can choose?" I asked, my voice a mere thought in the vast expanse.

In response, the pillars whispered, "Master, all is chosen."

I looked at the constellations of light, their paths inviting and mysterious. I reached out to touch one, feeling it move around my fingers like liquid stardust. As I closed my hand around the light, it was as if a door opened, revealing a glimpse of a new world.

I began touching the different pathways of light, each opening a doorway to new times, places, and spaces. One constellation showed me a bustling city in the distant future, its skyline filled with soaring towers. Another revealed a serene forest, ancient and untouched, its air filled with the songs of unknown creatures. Each path was a portal to a different reality, each more captivating than the last. The constellations weren't just destinations; they were stories waiting to be lived.

The pillars of light watched, their presence a constant reminder of the boundless choices before me. "Master, all is chosen," they echoed, guiding me gently.

I hesitated, a new question forming in my mind. "May I go back?"

Beneath me, a constellation of stars began to stir, moving together in a graceful, celestial dance. As they swirled and twinkled, a hum filled the air, a deep, resonant sound that grew in intensity. The stars collided in a brilliant burst of light, merging into the form of a majestic lion that burned bright with the colors of fire, its mane a blazing cascade of reds, oranges, and golds. Its eyes glowing like molten lava, fierce and knowing, as if it held the wisdom of the cosmos within them.

The lion began to walk away from me, its movements powerful and purposeful. As it strode forward, it left behind a trail, almost invisible to the naked eye, the thinnest and smallest of threads, glowing a faint red under the light of the twinkling stars.

As I followed the lion, the thread vibrated with each step, sending ripples of sound through the air, a hum, soft and almost imperceptible, like a whispering breeze. The hum grew louder as I drew closer to the lion, resonating with a deep, almost primordial rhythm that echoed through the empty space.

Suddenly, the lion stopped and turned around, its fierce eyes locking onto mine with an intensity that made the air crackle. Then it let out a thunderous roar, the sound reverberating through the void. Abruptly, the lion charged straight at me, its fiery form a blazing comet of light and heat. As it collided with me, flames erupted around my body, licking at my skin. But instead of burning, the fire fused with my essence, becoming part of me. It was as if it recognized me, accepted me, and claimed me as its own.

A fire ignited deep within my stomach, a core of blazing energy that pulsed with life, and the heat spread through my body, infusing every cell with a vibrant, almost overwhelming vitality. The flames roared within me. For a brief, eternal moment, I existed as something more than human, a being of flame and light.

Then, as swiftly as it had begun, the flames receded, and I found myself back in my body, staring at the fire in the tent. The logs had fallen into place, creating a perfect structure that allowed the flames to grow and thrive. The fire had intensified, its warmth spreading through the entire tent, flickering and dancing, casting a golden glow that bathed everything in a soft, welcoming light. The cold that had gripped me earlier was gone, replaced by a deep, soothing warmth. I took a deep breath, feeling the fire's energy still burning. My clothes, now dry and warm, lay near the fire, and I put them on slowly, savoring the comforting heat that clung to the fabric.

As I sat by the fire, the warmth wrapping around me like a comforting embrace, I stared into the flames. A flicker caught my eye. Within the fire, I saw a glint of light bouncing off the thin red thread that had led me back to this life.

Before long, the guide picked me up from the campsite. I climbed into the car, my mind a swirl of confusion—had it all been a dream? was I still dreaming?

As we made our way back to town, I stared out the window, lost in thought. Every now and then, I caught a glimpse of that red thread glistening in the sunlight, weaving through the wet, snow-covered streets.

When we made it back to town, my guide took me straight to a medical facility. I followed him, still in a daze, unsure if I was still caught in some dream. As we walked, my mind swirled with remnants of the surreal journey. Suddenly, my foot slipped on an icy patch of sidewalk, and I went crashing down. The impact was jarring, pain shooting up through my hip and back. It was a sharp, undeniable reminder of the reality I was now in—there was no pain in the place where things were made, only here in the physical world.

The guide quickly helped me to my feet, his grip steady and reassuring. We continued inside, where a nurse took my vitals.

"Did you see the Northern Lights?" she asked, her eyes full of curiosity.

"I did," I replied, the memory of their celestial dance still fresh in my mind.

"Were they out of this world?" she asked.

I wanted to answer, but I couldn't find the words to explain.

The experience was beyond the reach of language. I smiled, "Out of this world."

Chapter 11
The Remembering

In the aftermath of the Arctic, the world unveiled itself in a dimension I had never known. It was as if I had been handed the keys to doors that led to different spaces and times, along with the directions to find them. Each day was a blend of the familiar and the extraordinary, a dance between reality and the surreal.

When I looked into the mirror to braid my hair, if I stared too deeply into my eyes for too long, I'd be transported to a different life. The mirror became a portal, and my reflection dissolved into a tapestry of past incarnations. I saw myself as a healer in an ancient civilization, my hands moving with practiced grace as I tended to the sick under the glow of oil lamps. The scent of herbs and the soft murmurs of gratitude filled the air, wrapping me in a cloak of purpose and compassion.

In another blink, I was a murderer, my hands stained with blood, the weight of my deeds hanging heavy on my shoulders, the cold, unfeeling gaze of my reflection holding the pain of a thousand regrets.

I began to see the world with new eyes. Everywhere I looked, I saw a mesmerizing dance of particles and light swirling around people like the colors of the Northern Lights. Each movement and flicker of light told a story, revealing the unseen layers of their inner lives.

People at peace were wrapped in gentle, flowing ribbons of soft pastels, drifting lazily like a river on a Sunday afternoon. Those grappling with turmoil had lights flashing erratically, sharp bursts of red and orange zigzagging in chaotic patterns, mirroring the storm inside them. Moments of joy were marked by radiant swirls of gold and yellow, dancing with a lively, infectious energy that lit up the space around them. Around each person, these particles danced, their movements and colors painting a vivid picture of emotions and experiences that words could never fully capture.

There were moments when I shook hands with strangers, and their touch became a portal to another time. In an instant, I saw flashes of our shared pasts—a hearty laugh exchanged in a bustling market, the aroma of spices filling the air around us, a solemn vow made under a vast, starlit sky, the universe itself bearing witness to our promise, a tearful goodbye at a train station, the clamor of engines and the scent of coal smoke lingering in the background.

In my sleep, I drifted to different worlds, each dream a vivid journey through time and space. The veil between my present self and the echoes of my past lives had been lifted. Each night, I found myself stepping into the shoes of my former selves, experiencing their lives with vivid clarity.

One night, I felt determination and fear coursing through my veins as a warrior, standing on the edge of a battlefield, the wood of my bow familiar in my hand. The air was thick with the scent of earth and sweat, and the distant sounds of clashing weapons echoed through the valley.

Another night, I was a healer in a bustling marketplace in medieval Europe. The air was filled with the rich aromas of spices and herbs. My hands moved deftly, mixing potions and tending to the sick, each gesture infused with a deep sense of purpose. I could feel the rough texture of parchment and the smoothness of glass vials beneath my fingertips.

Each dream was a portal to a past life, filled with details so vivid they left an indelible mark on my waking mind. The taste of victory, the smell of healing herbs, the sound of sacred chants—they all lingered with me, blurring the line between my current reality and the myriad lives I had once known. When I woke each morning, the remnants of past lives clung to me like a second skin. I was disoriented, trying to reconcile my present self with the multitude of identities I had inhabited.

In the years that followed, I continued to travel around the world, guided not by travel books or guides but by an unexplainable calling. It was as if my journey was orchestrated by a force beyond me. Perhaps it always had been, but now I recognized it with a clarity that was both unsettling and exhilarating.

It felt like a gravitational pull, an unseen force drawing me irresistibly toward certain destinations. At times, I was called to a place by a low hum, a deep, resonant sound that seemed to vibrate through my bones, beckoning me onward with its mysterious song. In quieter moments, I saw my path laid out before me as an almost invisible string, a delicate filament that shimmered red when I focused on it. The glimmering thread wove through my life, guiding me through bustling cities, serene landscapes, and ancient ruins.

Each destination held a piece of the puzzle. It was as if I were retrieving fragments of my soul, scattered across time and space. Each journey was a step toward wholeness, a slow and deliberate process of remembering. Like a person with amnesia, I was gradually piecing together the story of my existence, reclaiming the lost parts of myself and understanding the interconnectedness of my past, present, and future.

In the rolling hills of England, I found myself drawn to an ancient circle of stones. Visions of a past life as a druid filled my mind as I remembered rituals of harmony and balance with nature, the connection to the earth and sky.

In Kenya, amidst the vast savannahs, I met a tribe whose traditions were as old as the land itself. As I watched them dance around the fire, the rhythmic drumbeats and spirited movements stirred memories of a past life as a tribal warrior. The values of courage, community, and respect for wildlife resonated within me, a reminder of a time when every sunrise was a blessing and every animal was revered as a sacred being.

In the rural villages of Tanzania, I was welcomed with open arms. Participating in a traditional harvest ceremony, I recalled a past life as a farmer in these lands. Memories of working the earth, of seasons of both bounty and scarcity, flowed through me. This life taught me the importance of perseverance and the deep connection between people and the land that sustains them.

The vivid biodiversity in Costa Rica's dense rainforests brought back memories of a past life as a healer. I remembered using the rich variety of plants for healing and spiritual rituals.

In Hungary, I wandered the historic streets of Budapest, finding myself at an old thermal bath. The warmth of the mineral-rich waters triggered memories of another past life as a healer, using these very waters to cure ailments.

In Tuscany, I walked barefoot through the sprawling fields, recalling a past life as a farmer, a life deeply intertwined with the cycles of the earth and the rhythm of the seasons. My hands, once calloused from working the soil, seemed to remember the feel of the earth, the weight of the plow, and the satisfaction of a successful harvest

In the raw, volcanic landscapes of Iceland, memories of a past life as an explorer emerged. I remembered navigating treacherous seas and discovering new lands, a life of adventure and resilience in the face of the unknown.

In Jordan, walking under the vast canopy of desert stars at night, a flood of memories washed over me. As I trekked through the dunes, the sand whispering beneath my feet, I remembered life as a Bedouin, roaming these very deserts under the same endless sky.

As I journeyed from one corner of the world to another, each destination became more than a mere pin on a map: they were waypoints on a spiritual odyssey.

Chapter 12
Breath

Everywhere I went, with each life I recalled, it felt like uncovering another piece of the puzzle. But despite all the pieces I gathered, I struggled to see the whole picture. I couldn't figure out how all the fragments fit together. What was the point of it all? This question became a silent companion on my travels, whispering in the back of my mind, urging me onward. It was this quest for understanding that called me to India.

Varanasi, the ancient city on the banks of the Ganges River, welcomed me with its lively streets, sacred temples, and the ever-present scent of incense. The Ganges flowed serenely, its waters carrying the prayers and ashes of countless souls seeking liberation. Here, life and death coexisted in a dance of eternal rhythm, offering a glimpse into the mysteries I sought to unravel.

In Varanasi, I studied under a revered guru, a man whose wisdom seemed to transcend time. His presence was both comforting and intimidating, a beacon of knowledge and spiritual depth. Our paths crossed in an ashram. In a dimly lit room adorned with relics and statutes of Hindu gods, the guru showed me a collection of human skulls, gifts from those seeking his blessings. He handed the skulls to me one by one. As I cradled them in my hands, I began to speak, recounting the life of the soul that once inhabited it—tales of love, loss, and longing flowed from my lips.

The guru watched silently, his eyes filled with recognition and quiet affirmation. When I finished, he nodded slowly, a knowing smile on his lips. "India is in your blood," he said, his voice a deep, resonant whisper.

Under the guru's guidance, I discovered how to harness the power of my own breath and energy. Each breath was more than just air; it was a bridge to the infinite energy of the universe. In the days that followed, the guru taught me how to control my breath, feel its rhythm, and understand its flow.

Before the greatest cosmic powers unfolded, the guru emphasized the importance of having a humble heart and quiet mind, becoming a clear, unobstructed channel for something greater than myself to speak. Through deep meditation and focused intention, I learned to pierce the veils of time. I tapped into the limitless energies surrounding us, the very lifeblood of the universe.

There were moments when the power felt seductive, an intoxicating force that threatened to overwhelm me. Sometimes, I saw too much and felt too much, and it all became noise, chaotic chatter that drowned out the clarity I sought.

In those overwhelming moments, the guru's teachings became my anchor. We would sit for hours, breathing in unison, as he showed me how to sift through the noise to find the quiet center amidst the storm. His voice was calm and steady as he instructed me to let go of the urge to control, to simply be a vessel through which the energy could flow.

On my last day with the guru, we sat in his modest kitchen, savoring pastries he had baked himself. Baking was his secret passion, a simple joy amidst the spiritual pursuits.

"Where will you go next on your travels?" he asked, his eyes twinkling with curiosity.

"I don't know," I admitted. "It's like answering a call. I go wherever it leads me, but I'm not sure where or why."

The guru smiled knowingly. "Long ago, we were all gods. But the chief gods watched with heavy hearts as humans misused their divine gifts. Brahma, the creator, called a council of the chief gods to find a solution. They pondered where to conceal the divine essence so it would remain untouched by human folly.

"'Shall we hide it in the towering mountains?' one god suggested.

"'No,' Brahma replied, 'humans are adventurous and will climb even the highest peaks.'

"'Shall we place it in the depths of the ocean?' another proposed.

"'No,' Brahma said, 'Humans are curious and will plunge into the deepest seas.'

"They deliberated, their minds seeking a place so hidden that humans would overlook it. Finally, Brahma decided. 'We shall hide the divine essence within their very hearts. There, buried deep, humans will seldom think to search.' And so, it was decided. The gods placed the spark of the divine within the core of every human soul, hidden in the quiet sanctum of the heart, waiting to be discovered."

He paused, letting the story sink in.

Offering me a pastry, he continued, "When you go to a restaurant, you must order what you want to get what you want. You will find what you're looking for if you ask for it. Call it by its name."

I stared at him in silence, feeling the weight of his words. He looked at me with gentle intensity. "You may be searching for adventure. You may be searching for truth. You may be searching for love. But call it by its real name."

His eyes held mine, unwavering, as if he could see the very moment his wisdom took root within me. "My girl, you are searching for God."

Chapter 13
God

The flight to Colombia was a mix of anticipation and trepidation as I made my way to participate in an ayahuasca ceremony. Ayahuasca, a sacred psychedelic brew revered for centuries by indigenous cultures in South America, was known for its transformative powers. It was said to be a gateway to inner worlds, offering insights and healing to those brave enough to partake in its mysteries. I had heard stories about ayahuasca ceremonies, of its power to induce an ego-death, a grueling but life-changing journey.

Healing and self-discovery weren't new to me—years of counseling, dozens of self-help books, and a toolkit of spiritual practices had been my steady companions. I assumed that all my years of healing prepared me for an easy journey, where I could simply speak with God.

I was wrong.

In the heart of the jungle, with the shaman and indigenous healers surrounding me, I brought the cup of ayahuasca to my lips. I was immediately struck by the brew's pungent scent, a complex mix of the jungle's deep, musky earthiness. The first sip was intensely bitter, with a richness that coated my tongue, leaving a tannin-like aftertaste.

The visions started slowly, just a gentle swirl of colors and shapes dancing at the edge of my consciousness. But then, like a storm building on the horizon, they intensified, pulling me down into the deepest recesses of my mind. Every forgotten corner, every hidden shadow came alive. I saw all the ways my old pains, shadows, and traumas still lingered in my bones.

I had convinced myself that I'd moved past rape and abuse. I had friends and lovers. I no longer flinched when touched. But ayahuasca peeled back the layers of my denial, revealing the stark truth. The medicine showed me how mistrust still lingered like a ghost, how I kept people at arm's length, never allowing myself to be truly seen. The abuse had woven itself into the very fabric of my existence, like a thread of darkness running through the tapestry of my life.

I saw how I had built walls, strong and high, to protect myself. I saw the way my body tensed, the way my eyes avoided contact, the way my heart remained guarded. The trauma had seeped into my bones, settled into my muscles, and taken root in my soul. It wasn't just a memory—it was a living, breathing part of me, influencing every decision, every relationship, and every moment.

Visions of my life flashed before me, raw and unfiltered. I saw how my entire life as a picture-perfect successful lawyer had been constructed on a feeble foundation of unworthiness, a constant feeling of never being good enough. The relentless pursuit of goals and achievements, the polished veneer of politeness and perfection—it was all a carefully crafted façade. Beneath the surface of my tailored suits and confident smiles, deep-seated shame festered like a rotting wound.

My gifts—to hear whispers beyond the ordinary, to smell the essence of places and people, to see into the unseen realms—had been buried deep within me. Shame had coursed through my veins like a toxin, tainting my perception and silencing my true self.

With each wave of nausea, my body convulsed, shaking out the poison of my past. The false beliefs that had shaped my life, the chains that had bound my soul, came rushing out in torrents of dark sludge. I was vomiting up years of pain and self-doubt, the bile a bitter, physical manifestation of the lies I'd been living. Each retch was a release, a purge of the toxic shame that had been coursing through my veins.

When the final wave passed, I collapsed, exhausted but finally unburdened. My body felt lighter, as if a great weight had been lifted. A massive boulder rolled off my shoulders. Every muscle relaxed, no longer tense with the burden of hidden pain. My mind was clear, like a fog had lifted, revealing the bright, blue sky of my thoughts. My spirit felt unchained, soaring high and unencumbered. I was clean, light, and free—reborn from the ashes of my former self.

As I lay in the grass, gazing up at the endless expanse of the sky, visions of my travels began to dance before my eyes. I saw the faces of people I met along the way, each one vivid and alive, pulling me back into moments of past encounters and conversations. I slowed my visions, studying closely, looking deeply into the eyes of each face. Within each person, I saw a flicker of light, a spark of the divine. Within each person, I saw God.

Their eyes held a light that spoke of ancient wisdom. Their smiles radiated a warmth that transcended love. Every act of kindness was a sacred gesture, every shared laugh a harmonious note in the symphony of existence. The ordinary moments of life were imbued with a hidden holiness, each one revealing the divine essence woven into the fabric of humanity.

I felt like I had journeyed through life lost, without direction, wandering aimlessly through a maze of experiences. I believed I was alone, fighting my battles in solitude. But as these visions unfolded, I realized the truth. Loneliness and separation were an illusion. Through strangers, whose paths fortuitously crossed mine along my journey, God had been walking with me. The divine had been my constant companion, lighting my path even when I couldn't see it. Every kindness extended, every grace received, and every friendship formed was a whisper from the divine.

As the visions continued, I found myself standing in a serene, softly-lit office. Before me, a person sat on a couch, tears streaming down their face as they unburdened their pain. I watched, feeling their anguish and sorrow, their need for understanding and peace.

I glanced around the room, taking in the surroundings. There was a wall decorated with a collection of framed pictures, in the center a picture of the Northern Lights. Soft music played faintly in the background. My eyes were drawn to a series of certifications and diplomas hanging prominently on one wall. My name was inscribed on each one.

Confusion washed over me. Was this my office? I was a lawyer. The only person who had ever cried in my office was me. What was this vision trying to tell me? As I stood there, searching for answers, a voice from beyond spoke with gentle clarity.

"This is your path," it said.

"What is it?" I asked, my voice trembling with uncertainty.

The answer came with a sense of calm and purpose: "You are guiding people to the light, their light."

I had been given the gift of sight, visions not limited to glimpses of the past and future. I could see into the very hearts of those before me, perceiving the divine. Despite the layers of pain and suffering that often obscured it, within each person, I saw God.

The voice spoke once more, its words resonating deeply within every cell of my body, "You will help them remember."

As the visions began to fade, I felt myself being gently pulled back to reality. The world around me reasserted itself, the sounds of the jungle returning to my ears, the earthy scent of the dirt and trees grounding me. I took a deep breath, feeling the solidity of the ground beneath me, and picked myself up from where I had been lying.

My body was heavy with exhaustion, but my spirit felt lighter than ever. I made my way to the small sink, turning the tap and letting the cool water flow over my hands. As I splashed it onto my face, the sensation both refreshing and grounding, washed away the remnants of the journey I had just experienced.

When I looked up, my gaze met the reflection in the mirror. For a moment, I hesitated, expecting to see the familiar face I had always scrutinized so critically. In the past, I had only looked into the mirror to fix myself, to make myself presentable to the world, dissecting every flaw and imperfection with a harsh eye.

But now, something was different. Within the deep, dark brown eyes staring back at me, I saw a depth I had never noticed before. I smiled at the reflection, a genuine smile, and whispered a silent thank you. For the first time, instead of seeing every flaw, I saw my eternal loveliness. I saw God.

Chapter 14
The Calling

In the days following the ayahuasca ceremony, I was compelled to write. For two days, I poured my heart and soul onto the pages, reliving my psychedelic journey and the insights it had bestowed upon me. When the final word was written, I stared at the manuscript, feeling a mix of exhilaration and uncertainty. The manuscript was raw, real, and full of my soul, but what was next?

My dog lay beside me, sensing my restlessness. I absently petted her soft fur, lost in thought. Then, as if carried on a breeze, the scent of lavender London Fog tea filled my senses, a soothing blend of bergamot, sweet vanilla, and calming lavender. Hoping a change of scenery might bring some clarity, I grabbed my laptop and headed to my favorite coffee shop for a cup of tea.

As I settled into a cozy corner with a steaming cup, I opened the manuscript on my laptop. The aroma of bergamot and vanilla mingled with the soft chatter around the coffee shop. Staring at the words on my laptop, I overheard a conversation at the next table that caught my attention.

Unable to resist, I walked over and introduced myself, explaining that I had just finished writing, but I didn't know how words on pages transformed into an actual book. The man, Phung, and his friend, Amy, offered me a seat at their table. Phung helped authors market their books and was in the process of finishing his first book. Beside him was Amy, a seasoned book writing coach with a knack for turning dreams into reality. Phung's eyes lit up with enthusiasm as he shared his journey, and Amy's warm smile radiated encouragement. The universe perfectly orchestrated everything, bringing me to the right place, to the right people, at the exact right time.

With their help and encouragement, "Rebirth of a Sage," transformed from a raw manuscript to a published book. It became more than just printed pages. It was a powerful catalyst, opening doors to new opportunities. No longer confined to the courtroom, arguing before judges and juries, I spoke on stages, using my voice to inspire those journeying in the darkness.

I knew I had a calling, a magnetic pull toward something greater, but I had no idea what to do about it. I didn't have a clear roadmap, but I knew I had to start somewhere. In the same way I poured my soul into writing my story, beginning was all that mattered. I was uncertain and unsure, but as I moved forward, the path revealed itself one step at a time. The universe responded to my courage by opening doors and serendipitous encounters with mentors who guided my way.

I returned to school to become a hypnotherapist, helping people transform their lives in ways they never thought possible. People came to me seeking healing, often with a vague sense of longing, unsure of what exactly they were searching for. Although they sought a healer to mend their perceived brokenness, I saw them in their wholeness. There was nothing to be fixed, no flaw or fracture that needed repair. They simply needed to remember their infinite power, a reservoir of strength and wisdom just waiting to be reclaimed.

Witnessing their transformations, seeing their remembrance of the divine within, filled me with a sense of purpose that was unparalleled. And yet, I still clung to my identity and job as a lawyer.

My days were a whirlwind of contrasting worlds. In one hour, I was fiercely debating legal points with opposing counsel, immersed in the logic and precision of the law. In the next, I was guiding someone through their trauma. One day, I stood before a judge and jury at trial, advocating for corporations with all the rigor and intensity my legal training had instilled in me. The next day, I was back in my healing space, helping someone uncover and release ancestral trauma buried deep within their DNA.

The transitions were jarring. One moment, I was in the structured, analytical environment of the courtroom, and the next, I was delving into the ethereal, intuitive realm of healing. The two worlds felt like they were in constant conflict, each pulling me in a different direction. Yet, I couldn't let go of either. My legal career was my foundation, my anchor in the material world. But my healing work was my passion, my truest calling.

The constant back-and-forth left me depleted, and my sleep became a battleground. Just as I was trapped between the different worlds while awake, in my sleep, I raced through past lives. Instead of finding rest, the wisdom of past lives screamed at me, raging with an intensity that was impossible to ignore. It was as if these ancient voices, each carrying the weight of their own stories, were desperate to ensure that I wouldn't repeat the mistakes of the past. They demanded to be heard and seen in this life, their lessons and insights pressing on me with a fierce urgency.

Each night, I found myself reliving pivotal moments from past lives, where choices and actions had led to joy or suffering, triumph or tragedy. The pull of these lives was relentless. They reached out with spectral hands, insisting that I heed their warnings and embrace their wisdom, making it clear that I was the custodian of their accumulated knowledge. They pleaded with me to carry forward their hard-earned wisdom.

In the mornings, I would wake up with a bloody nose, gripped by terror. In the first minutes of waking, I didn't know who I was, where I was, when I was, or sometimes what I was.

Desperate for guidance, I journeyed inward. In meditation, the noise of the world faded, replaced by silence and stillness, where clarity reigned and the truth whispered its secrets.

In this stillness, I repeatedly received an instruction that filled me with apprehension: one more big jump. I was urged to leap away from my old life and embrace a new one, but the destination remained shrouded in mystery. Whenever I meditated, vivid images of my hands tightly clenched would appear, symbolizing my grasp on control. I was urged to open my hands, to release my grip, to let go of the control I held so tightly and surrender to the unknown. The message was clear and unyielding, yet the fear of what lay beyond kept me tethered to my familiar reality.

Mediations brought back memories of stories I heard in church as a child, how it was easier for a camel to go through the eye of a needle than for a rich man to enter heaven. I was reminded of Abraham's deep yearning for a son and the ultimate test of his faith when God asked him to surrender the very child he cherished in exchange for the promise of becoming the father of many nations. These tales weren't just about sacrifice—they were about trust. They were tested on their ability to let go of what they thought was good in exchange for something even greater. They were lessons in faith, in trust, and in the willingness to jump into the unknown.

I slaved and sacrificed to become a lawyer. Endless nights of studying, grueling exams, and countless sacrifices had finally paid off. I was burdened with massive student loan debts and a mortgage that seemed to loom over me like a mountain. How could I possibly take that leap into the unknown, not knowing where I would land? The uncertainty was paralyzing.

Being a lawyer gave me security and safety in more ways than one. It was more than just a steady paycheck and a comfortable life. It offered me a well-defined path, clear rules, and a sense of order that I could depend on. It was the respect that came with the title of esquire. I wore my title like a badge of honor.

On the other hand, my healing practice was a step into something unpredictable, uncertain. People often dismissed it as voodoo or woo-woo, questioning its legitimacy. The healing world was filled with ambiguity and skepticism.

Yet still, in every meditation, the same message echoed in my mind: "One more big jump." Frustration gnawed at me, growing each day as I heard nothing beyond this single, persistent instruction.

Finally, exasperated, I shouted into the abyss, "But I am safe!" My words reverberated around me, fading into silence.

An image began to materialize. I saw myself bound by heavy chains, their links thick and unyielding, each one representing a fear or doubt. The constricting shackles around my wrists and ankles were cold and heavy, biting into my skin, symbolizing the burdens and limitations I had imposed upon myself. In my hand, a key glimmered with a faint, hopeful light, offering a promise of freedom. I was in a prison of my own making.

Gently, the abyss responded, "But are you free?"

Chapter 15
The Beginning

My parents were born into poverty in the Philippines. My father, the youngest of ten siblings, often reminisced about the lengths they went to find simple pleasures. He and his older brother would use broken pieces of mirror to catch fleeting glimpses of the neighbor's television, the moving images a tantalizing escape from their reality.

He painted vivid pictures of their foraging missions at the local YMCA's garbage, where they scavenged for anything of use. The most useful finds were the discarded, stained towels tossed aside by others but treasured by his family. These worn, threadbare rags became their bedding and blankets, spread out on the cold concrete floor where they lay their heads each night.

My mother was the third of seven children and the eldest daughter, a position that came with its own set of responsibilities. In her early years, she lived in a home without electricity or indoor plumbing. From the moment she could walk and talk, she was by her mother's side, helping to sell eggs in the marketplace.

My mother had an insatiable thirst for knowledge. Without a clock to guide her, she knew it was time for school when she saw the other children making their way down the dusty road. My grandmother recognized a spark in her that set her apart and saw my mother's brilliance and potential. Despite the family's daily struggle to put food on the table, she managed to surprise my mother with a bookbag, a rare and precious gift.

One evening, as my mother was hunched over her books, studying by the dim, flickering candlelight, the candle toppled over, and the flame caught the edge of the bookbag. In moments, the fire consumed it, turning her most cherished possession into ash. That bag hadn't just been a container for her books; it'd been an expression of her mother's faith in her.

Both of my parents worked relentlessly, pushing through barriers and defying the odds to make their way to college. My father pursued mechanical engineering, carving a path in a field that demanded precision and skill. My mother, undeterred by the male-dominated industry, became a chemical engineer, breaking stereotypes with every step.

As a child, I remember sitting with my father and asking him what he wanted to be when he grew up. He looked at me with nostalgia and said, "I wanted to be a doctor and build a hospital for people who couldn't afford medical care."

My young mind couldn't understand. "Why didn't you become a doctor?" I asked, confusion furrowing my brow.

He explained that in the Philippines, becoming a doctor was a privilege reserved for the wealthy. No matter how hard you worked, some dreams were simply out of reach. My mother shared a similar story, often recounting her love for numbers and her aspiration to be an accountant, another career closed off to her by the financial limitations of her family.

My father's voice would soften as he explained why they made the monumental decision to immigrate to America. "We came here so that you and your sister could be anything you wanted to be," he'd say, his eyes reflecting a deep, unwavering hope.

They sacrificed everything familiar and dear to give us the freedom to dream without bounds. Their journey wasn't just about escaping poverty; it was about opening doors for their children that had always been closed to them.

In one of my astral travels, beyond the confines of time and space, I journeyed to a moment where my parents existed in their youth, long before I was born. I observed them from a distance, their faces unlined by the struggles of life, their spirits unburdened and brimming with vitality and purpose.

I saw my father, young and full of dreams, his eyes reflecting a determination that could move mountains. He carried himself with quiet confidence, already beginning to envision a future where he could transcend the limits imposed upon him by his birth. My mother, too, was a beacon of strength and intellect, her love for learning shining brightly even amidst the hardships. She moved with grace and resolve, her mind always working, always planning, dreaming of a life where she could make her mark.

In that ethereal space, I saw that I had chosen my parents, and I knew exactly why. They were visionaries. In their own way, they possessed an ability to see beyond—to believe in a future that was better than their present. Their circumstances may have been harsh, but their spirits were unyielding, their dreams indomitable.

Though my parents held respectable jobs as engineers in the Philippines, they chose to give it all up when they immigrated to America, bringing me at the age of two and my sister at the age of six. The move was a leap of faith, one made even more daunting by our status as illegal immigrants. Their college degrees, hard-earned and cherished, were suddenly worthless in America.

Undeterred, they took on any job they could find, often working three jobs at a time to make ends meet. My father, who once worked as an engineer, now labored at a dry cleaner's and a gas station. On weekends, I joined him on his newspaper delivery routes, watching the early morning light break over the horizon as we tossed papers onto doorsteps. Despite the exhausting grind, they never complained. They bore the weight of their sacrifices with quiet dignity, their eyes always fixed on a brighter future.

After decades of relentless work and sacrifice, my parents finally made it. We moved out of the tiny apartments in rough neighborhoods and into a home of our own. My parents returned to school, determined to achieve their dreams. We became American citizens.

My parents didn't just survive; they thrived. They became successful entrepreneurs, building a business with the same tenacity and vision that had carried them through their hardest days. They transformed the American dream into their reality, showing my sister and me that anything is possible.

Decades later, I found myself standing on a precipice, paralyzed by fear. My parents had given up everything they knew, moving to America with broken English and no guarantee of success. And here I was, afraid to shift careers, clinging to the comfortable and stable life I had built. In the shadows of my parents' bravery, I felt like a coward.

Suffocating on my cowardice, I turned to my mother one day and asked, "When you gave everything up and moved to America, how did you do it?"

My mother, ever the pragmatic soul, began detailing the logistics of relocating and finding work. I interrupted, my voice trembling. "I don't want to be a lawyer anymore."

My words stunned her into silence. "Are you in trouble at work? Are you losing your job?"

"No," I assured her. "My business partner wants to retire soon, and he actually wants me to be the managing partner."

"Then what's the problem?" she asked, confusion and concern etching lines on her forehead.

"It feels empty," I confessed. "When I'm in court arguing over problems that feel so trivial, I feel like I'm wasting what time I have in this life."

My mother listened quietly, her eyes softening.

"I'm afraid. What if I fail? What if I don't make it? When you gave it all up and moved to America, how did you do it?" This time, she understood the depth of my question.

"Faith," she said softly. "A lot of determination. I never took no for an answer. And prayer. Humility. Trusting not in my power or plan but in God's. I prayed for things, but I always told God, 'If it is your will, thank You. If it's not your will, thank You.'"

I shared with her my struggles with sleep and how it had become such a problem that I was scheduled to be studied by sleep specialists. She reassured me, "There's nothing wrong with you."

"But it's not that I can't sleep," I explained. "In my sleep, I don't rest. I move through different times and spaces and wake up not knowing who, when, or where I am." This was an admission I never thought I would make, especially to my deeply religious mother.

To my surprise, my mother nodded. "It happens to me too sometimes. I dreamt of September 11 before it ever happened. Your dad woke me up from it. We were both shocked when my dream came true."

"I feel things. I know things. I smell things, like when people are sick," I continued, the admissions spilling out uncontrollably.

"So do I," my mother said calmly. "It is a gift."

"I don't know what to do," I admitted, feeling vulnerable and lost.

My mother smiled, "When God gives you the opportunity to live the life you want, you have to take it."

Her words hung in the air, heavy with meaning and love. Growing up, my parents had always emphasized success, pushing my sister and me to excel. But as I stood there, absorbing my mother's words, I understood that their ultimate desire for us was not measured in financial wealth or professional accolades. They wanted us to be fulfilled, to lead lives rich in purpose and faith.

"I believe in you," my mother said, her voice steady and full of love.

I smiled, imagining my grandmother saying the same words to my mother all those years ago. My grandmother might not have known just how much those words would mean, how far they would carry her daughter, and how much she would achieve. It was as if my grandmother had passed on a baton, entrusting my mother to go further than she ever could. Now, my mother was passing that same baton to me. I felt the weight of their collective dreams and the strength of their vision coursing through me. That belief had propelled my mother to incredible heights, and now it was my turn to take that leap of faith.

I had traveled the world only to find my way back home, realizing that the guidance I was seeking had been there all along. It was there in my parents' unwavering example and even in their very names. My mother, Luz, whose name means "light," illuminated the path through her perseverance and grace. My father was named after the biblical character Daniel, who had unrelenting faith even when a lion threatened his life. At the end of each day, no matter how little we had, my father would kneel in prayer, offering his gratitude to God.

Sometimes, the guidance we seek seems shrouded in mystery. Sometimes, God is a comedian and hides it in plain sight.

As I stood at the crossroads of my own journey, I realized that their legacy was my greatest source of guidance. The light my mother carried and the faith my father embodied were not just their strengths; they were my inheritance.

And so, I journeyed once again through meditation, returning to my inner kingdom. There, I confronted the haunting vision of myself, bound in thick chains and rusted shackles. I opened my hand, feeling the cool metal of the key that held my freedom. As the chains fell away, my clenched fists slowly unfurled.

In that moment of freedom, with my hands open and palms to the sky, I felt an unexpected warmth—a hand holding mine. I looked up to see a vision of my future self standing beside me, exuding an aura of strength and serenity. Her eyes sparkled with wisdom and compassion, and her smile was a beacon of hope. With her hand in mine, I felt the peace, purpose, and passion that flowed through her veins like fire. Her power was palpable, greater than my own, a testament to her true alignment. She gently held my right hand, her touch reassuring and filled with promise.

"Ready?" she asked, her voice a melodious blend of encouragement and certainty.

One more big leap.

As I jumped into the unknown, I realized I was not alone. To my right, my future self, who had navigated the path and knew the way, stood grateful that I had never given up. To my left was the little girl I once was, with wide-eyed innocence and boundless dreams, beaming with pride for the woman I had become.

Behind me were the many incarnations of my past lives, each carrying the accumulated wisdom, strength, and fortitude cultivated over lifetimes. My ancestors stood tall behind me as I leapt, their faces glowing with pride, witnessing the fruition of their sacrifices. Though their lives had been marked by poverty and hardship, they saw that their struggles had not been in vain. Their legacy of perseverance and resilience had paved the way for me to leap. I was their answered prayer.

I longed for a bigger life and could no longer keep fighting for a smaller one to stay. With my heart pounding and courage rising, I took that leap of faith—I resigned from my law firm. I let go of every trace of my perfect life plan, casting aside the illusion of control I had so meticulously crafted.

In my relentless pursuit to plan and predict every aspect of my life, I had been forcing my will, confining myself to a narrow path of my own making, unknowingly limiting the limitless. In surrendering to whatever may come, I invited the universe to guide me, trusting in its wisdom.

With the universe as my guide and intuition as my compass, I stepped into the unknown. The chaos that once frightened me now felt like fertile ground for creation.

Even stars are born from chaos, swirling clouds of gas and dust, ignited by force and pressure to give birth to a brilliant light in the universe. I was no different. Amidst the chaos, my light was reborn.

Epilogue

After roaming the world and dancing with both adventures and misadventures, everyone told me that I should write a book. Truth be told, this book nearly didn't see the light of day. I thought the script was supposed to go: eat, pray, then ride off into the sunset.

For a moment, I believed that this story wasn't worthy of being told, because the ending of this story, at least this chapter of my life, wasn't wrapped in a pretty bow and neatly packaged with a beautiful, easily digestible happily ever after.

Yet, here it is, because this story—this wild, untamed journey—matters. We often find ourselves stuck in the space between who we were and who we're striving to be. But in this space, there is power. There is beauty in the becoming.

In my journeys, I've met countless souls who, like me, were in search of something more, something deeper than the surface-level promises of fairy tales. We were all seeking a story that wasn't afraid to embrace the raw and the real, the messy and the magnificent. What I've come to realize is that the beauty of our stories lies not in their endings but in their unfolding.

This book is not a testament to a life perfectly lived but to a life fully experienced. It's a celebration of the moments in between, the lessons learned through trial and triumph, the love found in unexpected places, and the truth discovered in the quiet spaces of our hearts.

As you close these pages, I hope you take with you the understanding that our lives are not meant to be wrapped up neatly but to be lived boldly. Embrace the journey, cherish the process, and find joy in the ever-present now. There is no need for a happily ever after when you are passionately and purposefully living your truth, ever after.

Made in the USA
Columbia, SC
18 August 2024

e35d807d-3fbf-43bc-90c1-57a595cd940bR01